# No-Nonsense Digital Transformation

*A Step-by-Step Roadmap*

*for Your Digital Journey*

Michael Cantu

Kathy Kent Toney

A Kent Business Solutions Publication

ISBN: 9798201262655

Library of Congress Control Number: 2021915786

Kent Business Solutions, LLC

www.kent.solutions

# Dedication

The book is dedicated to business leaders who have struggled with past digital transformation initiatives or are just beginning and don't know where to start. We hope this book can help you have a more successful and profitable digital journey.

# What They Are Saying

Digital transformations are scary, 84% fail, and organizations have wasted over **$900 Billion** on poorly run projects by Fortune 100 Companies. But with Michael Cantu and Kathy Kent Toney's new book "No-Nonsense Digital Transformation: A Step-By-Step Roadmap for Your Digital Journey," you can take the plunge with confidence. It gives clear step-by-step guidance on how to deliver a successful digital transformation. This book tells you everything you need to know to avoid the common pitfalls and set yourself up to join the 16% of successful projects. Not only does it tell you how to do it, but it explains it in a way that is easy to understand and implement. I highly recommend it.

**- Gordon Tredgold – Global Guru Top 10 Leadership Expert and Speaker**

Digital transformation has many meanings, many sources of disappointment, and many sources of outright failure. This book provides the starting point for addressing the seeds of dissatisfaction and then provides a step-by-step process for increasing the probability of success for your digital transformation project. The no-code approach described by Michael and Kathy removes many barriers to digital transformation success, such as preventing the integration of the many systems needed to move the business into a seamless provider of digital products or services. They describe the planning steps required to increase the probability of success for the transformation project, starting with the software that enables transformation and this software's impact on the cultural shift needed to receive the business and technical benefits. In this short book, Michael and Kathy guide you through the top-level steps required to deliver a successful digital transformation project to accelerate your firm into a modern world of seamless productivity.

**- Glen Alleman, MSSM, USC – Keynote/Invited Speaker, Master Class Delivery for SW Intensive System of Systems to the U.S. Government**

This book is an excellent blueprint for any business leader serious about undertaking a digital transformation (DX) initiative. Michael and Kathy dive deeper than the digital enablement software tools required for effective transformation and get to the heart of the mindset and cultural changes it takes to achieve demonstrable productivity gains. For any company whose most significant asset is its people, the blueprint provides constructive models for engaging them in planning and execution processes, designed to better equip the team for high productivity and innovation. Coupled with the technological advantages of the highlighted **Accelerate** platform, this book will provide invaluable guidance to all who follow it. I highly recommend this guide for any digital transformation initiatives.

**- Allen Cantwell, Managing Director, Inveniam Group - a boutique transformation consultancy**

**No-Nonsense Digital Transformation** is a highly valuable guidebook for anyone looking to start a digital transformation project. It provides clear and concise real-world guidance on the benefits, pitfalls, and best approach for implementation. Throughout the book, you will find highly valuable "nuggets" of best practice suggestions. Dig in and enjoy!

**- George Commons, Global Sales Leader – AI & Business Automation**

# Acknowledgments

## From Michael:

**Kathy Kent Toney** – thank you for your inspiration and consistency in working together to develop something that can add value to many different people. Without your skills and expertise, this book would not have been possible.

**Alexander Steffanell** – for encouraging me to be the best person I can be. My contribution to this book reflects a large part of my worldview on working well with others and encouraging others to grow and be their best, much of which I learned from you.

## From Kathy:

This book would not have been possible without the help of my incredible friends and business colleagues, too many to name, so THANK YOU!

*Special thanks go out to:*

**Michael Cantu** – thank you for letting me download and put into words all the wisdom and digital transformation expertise that lives in that brain of yours. This book would not have been possible without you. Also, thank you for all your encouragement and for being a true pleasure to work with.

**Breandan Filbert**, my sales coach – thank you for encouraging me to start my writing journey and continually pushing me to accomplish big things, like writing this book. Thank you also for the chain of introductions that resulted in my connection to Michael.

**Gordon Tredgold, Glen Alleman, George Commons, Tom Witty, Allen Caldwell, Frank Armato, and David Leavitt** – thank you for your suggestions to improve this book.

**Robert Kent**, my content editor - thank you for rescuing me from the editing nightmare I faced with publishing this book. Your efforts proved invaluable.

Last but not least, I want to thank **God** for giving me the opportunity and skill to write this book!


Layout and Cover Design: Kathy Kent Toney and Ben Orcutt

# Table of Contents

# Introduction

Imagine this: you're a business leader that uses information technology as a critical contribution to their business operations. You're facing a multitude of challenges:

- Employees burdened with excessive manual tasks

- Non-productive work due to employee errors

- Antiquated IT systems that don't communicate with each other

- Poor customer experiences

- Wasteful business processes

- Disengaged employees

The next question is: how are you going to solve these challenges?

The best answer is **Digital Transformation (DX)**. It can solve these issues, and there's lots of evidence to support this assertion.

Take Sophos, a global cybersecurity solutions company of +3,000 employees. They had recently implemented Salesforce, and their end-users struggled to keep up with new customizations and processes, resulting in a significant increase in support tickets. They partnered with Whatfix to provide digital employee training and in-app guidance for their employees. Post-implementation, they experienced the following annual gains: 15% (~12,000) global reduction in support tickets; user satisfaction score of 9/10; 1070 employee hours saved; and an ROI of 342%.

This case study is just one example of the power of DX to transform businesses. Its importance grows with each passing day, and the savviest CIOs and business leaders recognize this. A recent Gallup survey discovered that 60% of executives have line items in their budgets for purchasing virtual tools.

And yet, many companies have been slow to embrace digital technologies. Take a look at Blockbuster—their refusal to do so obviously didn't end well!

For all these reasons, that's why Michael Cantu (a DX guru) and I (Kathy Kent Toney) wrote this book. Our goal was to provide a *no-nonsense roadmap* to help business leaders like you understand the power of DX and, at the same time, ensure that it can work for you. We also want to answer commonly asked questions, discuss the benefits of DX, and lay out a best-practice roadmap to get started on your journey.

And Michael is indeed a DX guru. He's helped organize and develop multi-million-dollar platforms for organizations like UnitedHealth Group and 40% of US credit unions and banks.

As for me, I've participated in my share of transformations. I'm a Six Sigma Black Belt with over 25 years working in large companies like Northrop Grumman, Bayer Animal Health, and Honeywell. Throughout my career, I've helped organizations improve business processes, helped guide DX projects, and helped them achieve multi-million-dollar revenue increases. So, we know a few things about this subject!

At the end of the chapters, we've included some parting thoughts on that particular topic:

- See it in Action, or
- Words for the Wise

These are additional examples of successful DX efforts, key takeaways, or a good dose of seasoned advice.

We've also included some *Reflection Questions* at the end of each chapter so you can apply what you've learned to your organization. There's plenty of room to jot down your ideas under each question in the book.

Ultimately, our goal is to help YOU on your digital journey. We hope you enjoy the ride!

# Chapter 1

## Digital Transformation—What's in it For Me?

> **What You Will Learn in This Chapter:**
>
> - *Definition of Digital Transformation (DX)*
> - *Definition of workflow automation*
> - *How workflow automation can be applied to various organizational functions*
> - *How DX can help with staffing challenges and disengaged employees*
> - *The reasons why organizations get started with DX initiatives*

**M**ost business leaders have heard the term ***Digital Transformation (DX)*** before, but what exactly does it mean, and how can it benefit companies?

Just so we're all on the same page, let's start with a clear definition of DX:

**It's the adoption of digital workflows and technology to replace manual, non-connected processes. It also involves building interconnected systems that take care of themselves across time.**

You may have also heard of workflow automation, which is sometimes used interchangeably with DX, but it's one of the overarching topics within DX. Let's also define workflow automation:

**It's the use of digital technology to perform a process or processes to accomplish a workflow function.**

The tool to perform this is *workflow automation software*. It expedites and enables organizations to connect disparate systems, people, data, content, and workloads to accelerate their workforce. It also streamlines work, allowing employees to have what they need to do their job at their fingertips.

In either case, the end goal is to create better service in companies that aligns business objectives for the future. It's about helping companies become more profitable and highly satisfying their customers.

Here are some examples of business areas that can benefit from workflow automation:

### 1. Accounting

An organization may be underutilizing its accounting system to the fullest extent possible, or there may be ways to digitally transform the workflow they have today. For example, they may receive invoices from vendors they could track more digitally than via email or paper mail. Doing so may enhance their existing systems. Or, they may want to implement an accounting system to address issues if they don't have one.

For instance, employees may be manually entering data from invoices or filing documents. Automating these tasks can free them to do more valuable work, such as increased client service. At the same time, you can improve accuracy and reduce the possibility of committing costly errors.

## 2. Business Acquisition

Many businesses have manual order or bid processes. Or perhaps it's all in someone's head, and that person has to teach the rest of the team members how to perform work. With little-to-no process controls inside of a bid system, the following problems can occur:

- Inaccurate bids resulting in lost business opportunities
- Overlooked tasks when scoping projects
- Improperly documented estimates resulting in lower margins
- Improperly ordered materials resulting in waste
- Redoing incorrect work

Ultimately, all these issues can result in unanticipated costs and negative impacts on the bottom line.

A way to digitally transform this part of the sales process is to bring in a new order or bid system. Companies can prevent these problems by having all orders or bids on one platform. Or, you can create digital workflows around handling approvals with an existing system. Having process controls and consistency in place can prevent many of these problems.

## 3. Solution Delivery

Once you win a bid, solution fulfillment needs to occur. You want to make this approach as brief and consistent as possible. For example, suppose your information collection is inconsistent, leading to incomplete customer information. That means you may have to contact your customer for more information you could have obtained upstream in the process.

You also want to ensure predictable process control so that the system can enhance decision-making instead of people remembering what steps to take. With these controls in place, the increased efficiency improves your quality through error reduction due to less human intervention. Doing so decreases cost and increases your margin. These gains also increase your data quality across your organization during the fulfillment process.

For example, if a new order is missing information, your team may have to jump back into the sales process to gather this info. This effort could be disjointed, requiring them to loop back into the process to fully document requirements. Doing so can cause resources to stand idle due to the delay because they can't start work, resulting in:

- Lost wages
- Project timeline delays
- Poor customer experience

Imagine this: you're a customer who thought your project or request was underway, and then you're being pestered for more information, perhaps multiple instances. That's not the way you want to treat your customers!

## 4. Customer Success

Business leaders often think customer success is at the end of the fulfillment spectrum; however, it occurs throughout the process. So how can digitizing workflows ensure the quality of output, namely the experience, is consistent?

Most customer success involves someone's ability to understand where a customer is in the process and convey that to them when they call in with issues. That also includes a follow-up cadence with the customer throughout the process. Technology allows you to implement those controls, from a customer success perspective, into workflows. For instance, automatically signaling when it's time to reach out to that customer on a particular matter is undoubtedly a good thing.

And what that does is keep your customer informed during the cycle.

But business leaders can do more to ensure excellent customer care. Here are several examples of how workflow automation can help achieve successful outcomes.

### *When Staffing Levels are Inadequate*

Many organizations struggle with maintaining adequate staffing needs; therefore, not having enough employees can negatively affect the ability to fulfill current orders and perform routine check-ins with the customer.

Automation can fill the gap by increasing employee efficiency. Reducing manual, often paper-based tasks minimizes the need for additional staff. An automated system can also perform follow-ups with the customer without any human intervention, such as text messages or emails notifying them of order status.

Or, if the company wants more one-on-one attention with customers, the system can notify employees when those interactions are required.

In the end, this increased efficiency and properly cadenced customer interactions can, in turn, increase customer satisfaction and retention. These positive outcomes are possible by establishing trackable metrics based on factual, real-time data, ensuring you make the right decisions at the right time.

### *When Staff Members are New or Disengaged*

Another benefit of workflow automation technology is this: many new employees, perhaps more apathetic ones, are not as attuned to highly satisfying customers. For the apathetic ones, their job may just be a job.

One of the best things about DX is that it can help sidestep potential problems resulting from employees who don't excel at highly satisfying customers. The previously mentioned automated emails or text messages are examples of how companies can prevent these problems from ever happening.

Automated customer success mechanisms can help solidify your customer experience by ensuring required interactions happen when needed so they keep coming back for more.

### 5. Document Digitization and Processing

This aspect gives organizations the ability, through automated workflows, to have the system extract all the information from documents instead of somebody manually reading the data and acting upon it.

At this point, a data entry person turns into a verification person. It allows the organization to get higher volume throughput by moving the data entry person to a higher knowledge center. That way, they can operate out of a higher part of themselves rather than just reading and copying information. When they can function out of a higher knowledge center, this improves the quality of incoming data because the system accuracy is very high. In addition, getting oversight from a data entry person for the revision makes the required activities much more straightforward.

## What Sparks Companies to Start their Transformation Journeys?

There are often two scenarios:

### 1. A Company Wants to Solve a Problem

Employees may be complaining about inefficient, archaic ways of doing their work. These efficiencies could be costing the company money or customers as well. Unfortunately, some are often overwhelmed by these problems, so innovation becomes just a pipe dream.

Many of these companies may have lots of innovative ideas, but being mired in these problems can outweigh the ability to implement their ideas. When issues like these are taken care of first, employees' capacity to think creatively often expands such that they have more freedom to start implementing these ideas.

## 2. A Company Doesn't Necessarily Have a Problem—They Want to Get Better

They may be unsure how to proceed or search for outside help within a price point they can afford. It may be a complicated conversation for many of them to start with consultants—it may not come easy admitting they don't have the answers to their challenges.

In the end, there are opportunities for both the business and the consultant to achieve positive results together. Here are some additional insights into how DX can fuel growth and innovation:

### *Business Stakeholders*

In our quickly changing world, it's impossible to know everything; however, when business stakeholders can accept this fact that's a great place to be. Organizations can often gain more understanding and value by seeking help or insight through consultants who are experts in their field.

Also, many companies may stop innovating due to uncertainty because it's human nature to relish solid parameters. However, if business leaders purposefully keep an open mind amid unknowns and push forward with their innovation plans, the capacity for their companies to keep innovating can increase. For example, 29% of executives at companies with high digital maturity reported DX's positive impact on growth and innovation (Deloitte 2020).

## *Consultants*

It's an opportunity for the consultant to have candid conversations with prospective and current clients while outlining what's possible. Organizations can benefit from having another set of eyes from outside the business to look at their operations, especially if they lack vital skills from within. This statement rings true when you consider a recent study by PwC. They found that 55% of employers experienced a slowdown in innovation due to insufficient in-house skills.

In these instances, the consultant's diverse experience allows them to quickly diagnose, suggest, and open opportunities for firms. Doing so can cause a positive trickle-down effect with their customers and, ultimately, the bottom line. What organization wouldn't want that?

**Words for the Wise: Digital Transformation is More Than Just Implementing Software**

There are two critical aspects of DX to embrace:

First, DX is a consistent effort to seek betterment *within* your process. For example, you've gone to the gym consistently and lost 20 pounds. You don't quit there. You have to keep going and eating right to stay fit, maintain your weight, or lose even more.

Second, it's an *essential* mindset. The best scenario happens when the service provider and customer actively participate in the conversation. We'll get into the importance of mindset in just a bit.

As a business leader, it's important to emphasize these two aspects throughout your organization. If you don't encourage your employees to continually improve and obtain the right mindset, getting stuck in old behavior patterns is a likely outcome.

***Reflection Questions:***

1. *What three things spoke to you while reading this chapter?*

---

---

---

---

---

2. *What is one thing you learned that impacts the way you view DX?*

---

---

---

---

---

# Chapter 2

## Benefits of Digital Transformation

**What You Will Learn in This Chapter:**

*How DX can:*

- *Increase efficiency*
- *Reduce manual tasks*
- *Increase quality*
- *Increase process transparency*
- *Minimize process breakdowns*

Business leaders can realize many benefits in their organizations through DX, which can erase years of experiencing inefficiencies and productivity losses, among other challenges. In a nutshell, the result can be streamlined operations that eliminate waste, reduce costs and ultimately increase profitability.

So let's dive a little bit deeper into these benefits.

### 1. Increased Efficiency Across Manual Processes

An organization may have standalone digital or paper documents and forms they're filling out for different items. Or maybe they're sending many emails back and forth between many people. After increasing the digital efficiency, they're experiencing more of an integrated approach, bringing awareness to what needs to happen next and accomplishing those things with less human intervention.

For instance, many data entry requirements can be replaced by digitally scanning documents into the system that automatically parses the necessary info to populate forms.

Work documents requiring review or signatures can also show up in an employee's work queue within the system, eliminating the need to email documents back and forth to employees.

## 2. Reduction in Manual Labor

Automated systems bring together correct documentation and tasks so people can do what they're supposed to be doing when they're supposed to be doing it. Doing so replaces multiple people manually making decisions and conveying information, which has more potential failure points. The benefit is reducing human failure by decreasing failure points in the process.

This error reduction aspect is also made possible through artificial intelligence and bots running in the automation platform's background that can make repetitive decisions on behalf of employees.

## 3. Increase in Quality

This benefit doesn't just involve quality products or services. It increases the quality of your relationships and customer satisfaction as well.

People are very good at introducing risk into manual processes because they forget to double or triple-check something. Mistakes that are missed and reach the customer will negatively impact that relationship and brand.

On the other hand, digital workflows have controls in place that automatically click in to reduce these mistakes. By tasks taking the same routes, digitally speaking, this removes the risk from your overall process. In addition, when errors occur, employees are more likely to catch them upstream— discovering these errors before they ever reach the customer. Doing so can help improve relationships with them and allow you to save on inventory, and reduce wasted effort. Ultimately, this combines to ensure customers have what they want when they want it.

## 4. Increased Transparency

When your team can see everything promptly, that's a huge benefit. In addition, this increased visibility reduces the possibility of potential process breakdowns.

Seeing everything when you need to see it is a big deal. Unfortunately, not all DX workflows allow for this to occur. Some service providers will only build you a digital form, which, by definition, is DX.

However, these limited types of projects still require team members to say something is incorrect throughout the process. Manually flagging issues is not the best-case scenario. You don't have an optimum workflow if you have too many emails going back and forth. Most people will read through the email strings and what's happened around something, but there's always the potential to miss something.

The ultimate experience involves this: when a system digitally places tasks right in front of your face and alerts you to that fact, including elevating potential issues and escalations to the proper level. Doing so leads to a better employee and customer experience.

Who wouldn't want that?

**See It in Action: Happier Patients and a Healthier Bottom Line—A Win-Win Scenario!**

Michael Cantu's cloud-based DX platform, **Accelerate**, has had success helping his clients to become more fit. Check out this case study of a behavioral health company he worked with:

*Problem*

Before the **Accelerate** implementation, his client's processes were inefficient and prone to user error. For example, employees were emailing hundreds of audit and financial forms back and forth to each other. There was also no central location for documents, which made it difficult to access them easily.

*Solution*

Post-implementation, **Accelerate** digitally coordinates all audits throughout the entire organization. Documents are centrally located and easily accessible to end-users through automated workflows or as-needed access. The system also tracks hierarchal approvals, so employees don't overlook customer billings.

*Results*

This organization has achieved a productivity increase of 200% and annual savings of $45K over the previous process. The developmental cost over other alternatives also resulted in a savings of $250K. One excellent outcome is improved patient care and reduced risk.

As you can see, DX can dramatically improve a firm's health and the bottom line. As a business leader, wouldn't you love to achieve that for your organization?

***Reflection Questions:***

1. *While reading this chapter, what two or three points resonated with you?*

2. *What is one thing you learned that impacts the way you view DX?*

# Chapter 3

## Business Agility and Digital Transformation

> **What You Will Learn in This Chapter:**
>
> *How DX can:*
>
> - *Simplify reassignment of tasks for unavailable staff*
> - *Transform employees into more of a knowledge worker*
> - *Provide objective data to measure employee performance*
> - *Improve efficiency and ensure compliance*

We've shared the benefits and efficiency gains of DX. Now, let's discuss how business leaders can mitigate risks by increasing the agility of their organizations. Doing so prepares organizations for times when disruption hits the three pillars of People, Processes, and Resources.

Some companies may encounter significant economic changes. As a result, they could be experiencing changes in staffing availability, disrupted supply chains, and even processes.

Automation can be a crucial tool for increasing agility to reallocate roles and gain efficiencies while maintaining two key areas that should be fundamental in all businesses: transparency and compliance.

Let's start with:

## 1. Role Allocation

During events like the COVID pandemic and changing economic landscapes, role allocation is something companies need to address due to:

- Unavailable staff

- Staff that are out intermittently

- The need to reallocate particular work items that bring higher value to the business

- Staff working from home

In such cases, an automation platform like **Accelerate** allows you to re-prioritize role allocation across your company with just a few mouse button clicks.

### *Unavailable Staff*

For example, a bank employee responsible for replacement cards or updating addresses is on leave. Their boss could have the ability to reallocate those roles to someone else within the organization quickly.

Another example is the remote employee who isn't pulling their weight. What's a manager to do about that? With **Accelerate**, you can drill down from your high-level team performance metrics to the employee level. That way, you can find out what tasks that employee has and hasn't accomplished that's been on their plate.

In a nutshell, workflow automation can provide objective data to managers that can be used for coaching purposes and help improve employee performance.

### *Higher-Level Functions*

One task of automation is to take lower-value duties and automate them. You can look for opportunities to manually remove or replace particular activities necessary for someone to do.

For instance, a particular employee could spend most of their time on data entry. But instead, management could assign that person to a higher-value activity, such as contacting customers to ensure they have what they want.

Automating those manual tasks enhances the employee experience to become more of a knowledge worker, which brings them to a higher-level function in the business.

Ultimately, this is where automation thrives by enhancing the overall experience for the employee and the customer, which can help achieve company goals.

## 2. Efficiency

We've already discussed this in a previous chapter, but we'd like to highlight another aspect of agility. It involves people, processes, and how you organize resources to accomplish the goal.

For example, let's say there's a particular process in the business that employees haven't evaluated for several years. Or, you haven't held a specific meeting with your team to see how the ordering of tasks could be better. They could be doing things that require a tremendous amount of time that's not allowing them to be agile.

Those meetings could improve efficiency, primarily if you utilize a tool that minimizes manual data entry in multiple systems.

## 3. Compliance

As you change your processes, you will want to ensure you integrate compliance into the automation pipeline. Doing so results in items getting done in a particular fashion, bringing consistency and quality repeatedly, and helping keep your company out of hot water with auditors.

## A Few Final Thoughts on Agility

Agility no longer has to do with just timing. Instead, it concerns your ability to quickly adapt to the current reality and let go of the prior state. Automation allows you to evolve.

You can still have the previous way of doing things, but you will modify targeted processes. So, for example, you can implement a new strategy and execute that strategy while also having the ability to go back to the old approach if you need to.

For instance, many companies had to change their supply chain strategy to survive the COVID pandemic. Post-pandemic, the ability to quickly return to their previous ways of doing business—without interruption to their operations—is an excellent approach.

Finally, you will want to include the ability to measure what you're trying to accomplish, which automation allows you to perform. Doing so will give you dashboards with real-time data at your fingertips, enabling you to make more informed, on-time decisions.

## Words for the Wise: Digital Transformation Doesn't Mean Losing the Human Touch

Many people think the DX wave sweeping our country will make employee and customer interactions seem more robotic. Fortunately, that's not the case!

The possibilities for more extraordinary and healthier levels of employee and customer interactions are conceivable. Employees can have more freedom to perform higher knowledge functions, such as more impactful customer communications, once multiple manual tasks disappear from their plates. In the end, higher levels of quality customer engagement can benefit the company.

Likewise, more frequent and improved employee interactions can occur. Just think of all the fantastic things employees will achieve together if given more time to accomplish them!

As a business leader, you may have to fight the urge to lay off employees due to increased efficiencies. But, if you decide to channel increased efficiencies in the right direction, you can improve the quality and levels of human touch within and outside your organization.

Now that you understand a little more about the benefits of DX, we'll discuss the different types of available software in the next chapter. We'll also discuss how affordable and accessible DX efforts can be for companies today.

*Reflection Questions:*

1.  *While reading this chapter, what two or three points resonated with you?*

   _______________________________________

   _______________________________________

   _______________________________________

   _______________________________________

   _______________________________________

2.  *What is one thing you learned that impacts the way you view DX?*

   _______________________________________

   _______________________________________

   _______________________________________

   _______________________________________

   _______________________________________

# Chapter 4

## Digital Enablement Software

***What You Will Learn in This Chapter:***

- *Definitions for three types of digital enablement software*
- *Benefits of no-code over other digital enablement software*
- *Four ways businesses can use no-code software*
- *How no-code software can increase efficiency, reduce costs, and optimize business operations*

Another cutting-edge benefit of DX is digital enablement software, which falls into three categories. Business leaders can benefit from all three, but one stands out from the pack.

Before we discuss this option in more detail, let's briefly review all three:

### 1. Ready-Made Solutions

Many of us are familiar with ready-made solutions, such as Microsoft Dynamics for sales functions or ERP solutions, like SAP or Oracle NetSuite. Even though they are mass-produced, they still require considerable time, resources, and dollars to implement within companies. Some of these implementations can take years!

## 2. Custom Solutions

These custom development solutions involve extensive coding to create a platform tailored to the customer's specifications. Like ready-made solutions, they require extensive investments in resources and money; however, timelines can be much longer and more expensive.

## 3. No-Code Software

No-code software is in a class of its own; it allows you to experience the benefits of a custom solution at a drastically reduced timeline and price tag for development.

It's important to note that few companies have taken advantage of the power associated with no-code software. For this very reason, business leaders that use this type of software can help propel their organizations forward in powerful ways. Let us explain how:

## No-Code Software

You may be asking—how can software be no-code? We're glad you asked!

A no-code development platform allows for building software applications without coding, allowing even non-technical employees to create their own applications. No-code platforms have a simple user interface that enables end-users to drag-and-drop elements to create the end product, such as an automated process or even a website.

On the other hand, programs created using traditional software development code can be challenging for businesses to change, leading to long development cycles and more considerable capital costs to meet business needs. Custom development software can also mean higher maintenance costs when it's necessary to change coding frameworks.

No-code software is beneficial because implementing workflow automation in a digitally saturated market can be extremely difficult due to a shortage of qualified IT specialists. So, no-code workflow automation software emerged to keep up with this increasing demand for change. Moreover, this emergence has benefitted many companies by eliminating large-maintenance nightmares.

No-code software accommodates an IT shortage, budget constraints, and timeline expectations. A user-friendly interface allows configuration from different teams within your company, giving all business departments access to automation. Doing so can unlock many possibilities through apps while making them readily available to your team members and customers.

Here are a couple of examples:

## 1. Accounting and Finance

No-code workflow automation software can speed up the work of your company's financial team. For example, you can incorporate profit and expense analysis and investment monitoring into a simple, automated workflow. On top of that, accounts receivable and payable collection can also be automated, including payroll and invoice reports.

One of the most reputable companies to automate their treasury functions is Rolls Royce. As a result, they experienced reduced data collection timelines from one month to four days in their financial systems (White Paper: Taking Automation to the Next Level – teknowlgy Group, 2019).

## 2. HR and Administration

Automating some HR and administrative workflows can be feasible using no-code apps, which often results in significantly reduced implementation timelines while still providing the same value as custom-developed solutions. Not only that, these platforms are considerably less expensive than custom options. You can also automate new hire onboarding and performance reviews to meet all your business needs on time.

One significant advantage of no-code software is the ability to create Key Performance Indicators (KPIs) and monitor remote worker performance. We touched on this in the previous chapter, but now let's dive into more detail.

When a particular employee completes a task, this updates the associated KPI in the automated system. An HR manager can then view the overall performance for that KPI and drill down to view the particular employee's performance. That way, they can objectively view their productivity against other team members. It's also important to note that this is factual data upon which a manager can gauge employee performance and make decisions. However, it is essential to remember that process problems often lead to performance problems. Fixing broken processes can often lead to improving employee performance.

Here's the key takeaway: no-code software allows for better training and enforcement of employee expectations because real-time, objective data becomes the basis for such activities. This ability becomes vital when evaluating remote worker performance.

## 3. Manufacturing

The manufacturing departments of businesses are no stranger to no-code workflow automation. Most companies utilize custom-made ERP and Excel data to manage their day-to-day operations. Due to shortened implementation timelines for no-code software, you can save time when prepping data and avoid custom-developing code to accommodate new processes.

Some common areas that could use no-code automation are order management, calculating production costs, quality assurance processing, and invoice preparation. You can automate all these areas with no-code workflow solutions.

**4. Sales and Marketing**

Implementation of no-code automation can be beneficial in streamlining sales and marketing campaigns. For example, building a campaign strategy can be simplified through quick, automated operations. You can classify data seamlessly to include in-depth analysis that measures ROI, sales and marketing assets, campaign reach, and more.

## Other Benefits

There are many benefits to no-code software, some of which overlap what we discussed in previous chapters, so we'll highlight two in more detail:

### *Increased Efficiency*

The current digital age extends the automating of workflows beyond the IT department. As previously mentioned, no-code SaaS platforms boost employee efficiency by allowing end-users to build automated workflows without IT assistance. Automating simple reminders, for example, can ensure that you accomplish specific tasks at the right time to avoid unnecessary delays and follow-ups.

Automation also bolsters employee productivity and job satisfaction. Removing dreadful administrative tasks from their plates gives them more time to prioritize the tasks that require their skills. Since workflows are available 24/7, sustainable performance is possible, allowing your company to meet demands, even during peak periods.

Furthermore, automation provides companies more opportunities to hone their employees' skill set, which keeps them satisfied instead of spending most of their energy trying to remember where they're at in a process and what they were doing.

### *Cost Savings*

Workflow automation generates savings by optimizing the way businesses run their entire operations. Time is money, making it crucial for companies to manage employee workflow effectively. As mentioned previously, automation reduces time and further enhances the capacity and agility of employees across different functions. In addition, once you correctly set up your automated processes, it eliminates mistakes due to human error.

### *Optimize End-to-End Operations*

Implementing no-code workflow automation is simple and impactful to the business's back- and front-facing end. For example, seasoned end-users of **Accelerate**, a no-code platform, can automate simple business processes in a matter of hours.

No-code software is also potent for minimizing work handling for small-scale, repetitive business processes. Doing so can develop uncaptured revenue. For example, customer follow-ups, validation of customer satisfaction, and providing offers to satisfied customers are examples of opportunities for optimization.

Workflow automation improves turnaround time for most online orders while reducing the number of employees needed to complete these tasks. For instance, self-checkout in stores minimizes problems of staffing shortages while improving efficiency.

As businesses evolve and embrace technological solutions, automation becomes an attractive option. No-code workflow automation software is emerging to provide a competitive edge while preserving technical resources for complex issues. It gives flexibility, extending its power to every department in your company without depending on IT professionals and additional resources. In addition, real-time solutions can instantly increase ROI and provide continuous improvement.

There are many possibilities made feasible by no-code workflow automation. So as a business leader, you could do yourself a big favor and consider no-code software when discussing digital enablement tools.

**See It in Action: Check Out These Astronomical Cost Savings!**

Here's an example of how **Accelerate** helped one client achieve significant cost savings on a project.

Their client, a transportation company, had a decentralized claims process that required frequent, multiple emails going back and forth to determine status.

In search of a solution, they reached out to one company and received a quote for approximately $1 million to develop a custom software development platform.

Ultimately, **Accelerate** won the deal because they could complete the same project for only $20K!

As this example shows, no-code software excels at saving money! Not only that, multiple **Accelerate** customers have achieved over a 300% increase in efficiency, so it's not just related to the initial investment.

As a leader in your organization, you could do your company a big favor by investing in this option to increase productivity and save money.

Now that you know more about DX, we'll explore how to plan for successful DX implementations in the following chapters.

*Reflection Questions:*

1. *While reading this chapter, what two or three points resonated with you?*

_______________________________________

_______________________________________

_______________________________________

_______________________________________

_______________________________________

2. *What did you learn about no-code software that impacts how you view DX and its possible role in your organization?*

_______________________________________

_______________________________________

_______________________________________

_______________________________________

# Chapter 5

## Transform Your Culture for Success

***What You Will Learn in This Chapter:***

- *Three things business leaders can do to transform their culture*
- *How to help ensure end-user acceptance of DX efforts*
- *How practicing radical acceptance of team members improves the likelihood of DX success*
- *How to deal with employees who are resistant to change*

Having the right culture that embraces DX is essential. Boston Consulting Group (BCG) proved this when they studied 40 digital transformations. BCG discovered this: organizations that emphasized culture were five times more apt to achieve breakthrough performance than those that ignored culture.

Yet, many business leaders are unsure how to create these types of cultures, and when they do nothing to address the issue, this can cause a project to fail before it starts.

So, what can business leaders do to create a culture that embraces DX efforts if they're not in that place?

There are three areas to focus on:

## 1. Encourage Your Team to Talk About Everyday Matters

Let your team members know there won't be any repercussions for discussing what's on their minds.

They should feel good about expressing their opinion. Companies do best when they've created a culture where employees can come to management anytime and discuss their concerns or ideas.

Unfortunately, there are many instances when top-level managers don't understand what's happening underneath. They know *what's* getting done or not getting done. But they also may not know *how* it's getting done or how people feel about their actions. So, giving them that safety net to do that is very important.

## 2. Create an Expectation You Will Be Asking Your Team for Feedback

Encourage them to explore better ways to do their jobs.

For instance, you can ask your employees their opinion on the best way to do something or if they've read books that gave them ideas on improving processes. By asking these questions, it helps them understand that their feedback is vital and requires them to participate in the business actively.

## 3. Act Upon Those Items

Talk with your employees about why you can't necessarily do what they're requesting right now. Then, make sure you give them a why.

You would still want to keep their suggestion as a viable option. Then the next instance, when you start reviewing those things, ask questions like:

- Do you still feel the same way about this item?

- Have you read about any additional solutions?

- Are we able to implement this together right now?

If the answers are "no," it remains active. However, if you can move the items forward, make it happen.

# Other Things to Think About

### *Radical Acceptance*

One over-arching aspect companies would do best to keep in mind is practicing radical acceptance of their employees. This discipline involves accepting each team member's uniqueness they bring to the table. Listening is key to understanding that everyone's different. Everyone has differing thoughts and ideas, and many fear voicing their opinions or beliefs. Therefore, it's essential to practice this idea of radical acceptance on an ongoing basis.

### *How to Handle People Stuck in Their Ways*

What happens when efforts to create this culture don't connect with employees who tend to be stuck in their ways and do not want to embrace DX? What do you do then?

The first step is to identify who these employees are so you can have one-on-one conversations with them. During these meetings, it's crucial to create a safe place for them so you can discover the reasons for their unwillingness to comply. You may be surprised to learn that some are willing to change. There may only be a disconnect in leaders' minds. Clearing up these misconceptions can prove helpful.

Next, ask them what you can do to help them become more adaptable to change. Some answers may be out of their control, but it's helpful if you can redirect them to what is within their power.

If they refuse to change, consider looking for replacements. Bringing in others who champion the type of culture you want can help make your DX efforts run smoother than otherwise.

Before you start replacing people, Michael Cantu has some advice:

"I've rarely seen anyone that has been closed off when you talk to them, from a managerial perspective, who didn't open up when they realized their job could be on the line. Either they have started looking for another job—because they don't want to change and do what's required—or they stepped up."

## See It in Action: How Do I Get These People to Change?

Here's a real-life example of how to handle employees who are stuck in their ways.

During Kathy's stint at a Fortune 100 company, she helped spearhead the implementation of a project management platform that replaced numerous manual processes. The organization launched the initiative with the expectation that all schedulers and program managers would use the system.

As expected, there were some resistant employees. However, the leaders were diligent about having one-on-ones with these employees to help them work through their resistance—all done to help ensure overall user acceptance of the software.

The result met their expectations—everyone was on board with the new software, and those who weren't (the resistant employees) either retired or left their roles for other positions. Having these one-on-ones works!

As a business leader, getting everyone on the same page is essential, even if it involves having tough conversations. Your organization is more likely to achieve a more significant buy-in of your DX efforts by doing so.

In the next chapter, we'll talk about how to overcome another closely related roadblock—having the wrong mindset.

*Reflection Questions:*

1. *While reading this chapter, which two or three points sparked ideas about implementing a culture that embraces DX?*

   ______________________________________

   ______________________________________

   ______________________________________

2. *What initiatives or ideas has your leadership team tried that didn't work for improving your culture?*

   ______________________________________

   ______________________________________

   ______________________________________

3. *What are one or two things you can plan to do to positively impact your culture on your next project?*

   ______________________________________

   ______________________________________

   ______________________________________

# Chapter 6

## The Importance of Mindset

*What You Will Learn in This Chapter:*

*The importance the following aspects have in creating the right collective mindset:*

- *Promoting a team-wide attitude of honesty and care*
- *Emphasizing team-wide endurance*
- *Ensuring visibility and transparency around team operations*
- *Defining change management efforts around DX initiatives*

A consistent, positive mindset is crucial for DX success. Business leaders who guide their employees to embrace such attitudes are more likely to help their organizations succeed. If they don't correctly address this aspect, naysayers and unresponsive employees can sabotage even the best plans.

The following statement best summarizes its importance:

**It's great to have a solid plan, good people, processes, and execution, but successful DX projects will be more challenging to achieve if you don't have the right mindset.**

The right mindset is the energy that keeps your project going. It's the idea that sustains your ideology.

Facilitating a great mindset starts with team members understanding the strengths and weaknesses they bring to a project. It also involves removing roadblocks that prevent the formation of a healthy perspective.

Here's an example of what that looks like:

Remarkable organizations are composed of individuals grounded in reality, goal-oriented, and know how to work well in a team. Teams function more effectively when they learn how to positively view change and the challenges they encounter as opportunities to overcome. They also understand the escalation paths they need to follow during their work.

These qualities are just the tip of the iceberg, so let's take a deeper dive into some other critical aspects of having a great mindset:

## 1. Honesty and Candor

Creating a mindset of honesty (always the best policy) and candor is crucial to successful teams, and team members should never devalue these qualities!

**Candor** involves naturally talking about things without negativity toward other team members. For example, when the team can discuss how to best complete tasks or how individuals can interact more effectively without finger-pointing, that's a good thing.

This approach also includes **Care**, which means having an attitude that you are all in this together. It involves determining how to best look after team members and knowing how individual members are doing.

Care comes down to active concern for the total person. Case in point—everybody has a life outside of work. The goal is to have an empathetic understanding of what employees are balancing so they feel free to share what they are experiencing.

Here's an illustration. Bob has been working late every night and seems stressed, which is uncommon for him. As a leader, it would be helpful to ask Bob how he's doing—to show genuine care to him and ensure he is doing all right. It may also involve "taking one for the team"— giving Bob permission to leave a couple of hours earlier the next day if that seems appropriate.

Here's another illustration of how having the right mindset throughout your team might appear: Bob's manager could ask someone to pick up the slack for him, and a team member would most likely be glad to jump in and help.

On the other hand, an unsupportive team mindset could result in many more problems on a project. Imagine this—team members with a fearful mindset will likely not be as forthcoming when something's a mess. Instead, they'll perhaps be more concerned about not meeting their work goals while caring less about the overall team goals. With that environment, it will be more challenging to find individuals wanting to jump in to help when someone needs a break.

Bottom line—it comes down to working with your team to build the right mindset, which helps create a healthier team culture.

## 2. Endurance

**Endurance** is another critical element of continued success and is a large part of having a great mindset. This staying power also includes focusing on what's most important to accomplish daily. Both factors are invaluable, whether you are building a business, a team, or your life.

Successful teams complete projects over and over again. Every day they come to work and complete tasks, finishing one more piece of the puzzle at a time. It has to do with their ability to endure. It involves team members keeping their mindsets positive and deciding to stay the course.

Of course, good leaders will use the "Care" approach by checking on team members to help them if they're getting stuck.

In the end, endurance is the ability to get up and do what it takes to realize measurable, incremental, and positive results that move you towards a successful project conclusion. It's also about making sure you do what you said you would do.

## 3. Visibility and Transparency

This aspect involves open communication with your stakeholders, both external and internal. Essentially, it's all about letting them know that you will have a mindset of honesty, candor, and care with them and that you will escalate issues when required. Doing so shows leadership how much you care about the project, which will most likely pay dividends throughout your work.

For example, if you miss a deadline, it may look less erratic when you raise the issue with management. It makes a difference in how leadership views you and the project.

Having visibility and transparency among all team members can positively affect the system's end-users and, eventually, the entire business. But that's not the only positive outcome. Creating an environment where open and honest communication flourishes among team members can help prevent roadblocks from impeding progress towards successful project completion, ultimately benefiting the company. We'll cover this topic in more detail later on in the book.

## 4. Change Management

Change management is about the behaviors and adoption of new processes and methodologies within an organization.

How you approach the communication of your organization's planned changes has a powerful effect on mindset. That's why a good change management approach is essential—employees in an organization need to understand what's changing. That way, they can prepare themselves for any changes to achieve the right mindset. In addition, effective communication of the effort required for a project to successfully transition from where they are to where they want to be is imperative. It's also about asking for their feedback along the way.

Doing so removes the outward perception of changing for change's sake and casts a future vision to help the organization succeed. Thus, it becomes an organizational change mindset.

This approach is vital because this can change the whole organization's attitude and help create a more accepting environment for DX efforts. That acceptance is critical to achieving success on your projects!

**Words for the Wise:  Envision Your Success**

A series of studies conducted by several heavy hitters (the likes of McKinsey, Oxford University, and KPMG) revealed the following statistic:

**70% of all respondents said they knew an IT project they were about to start would fail from the onset.**

So, here is our advice—establishing the right mindset in your organization by following the above steps is essential for success!

Better yet, following the steps in the upcoming chapters will also increase the likelihood of success on your digital projects.

That starts with the planning process, our next topic of discussion.

*Reflection Questions:*

1.  *What three points resonated with you around establishing a mindset that embraces DX?*

    _________________________________________

    _________________________________________

    _________________________________________

    _________________________________________

2.  *Of these three points, which one spoke to you the most?*

    _________________________________________

    _________________________________________

    _________________________________________

    _________________________________________

3.  *What one or two things can you implement to help improve the mindsets of your team?*

    _________________________________________

    _________________________________________

    _________________________________________

# Chapter 7

## Planning for Digital Transformation

Business leaders who have improved their organization's culture and collective mindsets are now ready for the next step—the planning process, a crucial element. Many DX efforts end up as unmitigated disasters resulting from not following proper planning guidelines. That's why having a robust plan is essential!

But before we jump into this topic, it's crucial to answer this question:

**Do I have key IT employees who are qualified to help in the planning process?**

**If not, skip to Chapter 8, which discusses how to create an exceptional team. After you've read that, you can jump back into this chapter.**

**Keep reading if you have IT employees who can help with this planning approach.**

There are four steps involved with this:

## 1. Conduct a Needs Assessment

This aspect involves an open conversation about the current state of the company.

It's often best to have an outside person doing these assessments so people feel comfortable in an anonymous kind of way; otherwise, your employees may not be forthcoming with their answers, which can skew data integrity.

Depending on the company's size, you can do this assessment within an individual department or company-wide. However, if you're shooting for enterprise-level implementations, you'll probably want to stick with a particular business unit.

If you're a medium-sized company, you can often have these meetings across all departments and start talking through the needs within the business.

## 2. Take an Inventory

This step involves getting solid support for the needs identified in the assessment. That includes going out to the floor—talking with other personnel, asking those questions, and looking at the organization's current state. Then bring the facts back to the table.

## 3. Prioritize the Change

Prioritizing the change involves analyzing the needs assessment results, including the collected data and the identified needs. Next, schedule a meeting in which you'll prioritize what changes you want to take place.

During the prioritization phase, list the potential change initiatives using population and revenue impact as inputs. Population impact concerns how many people are impacted by this change and why your company needs to start undertaking it. Then pull this data forward to the next step.

## 4. Make an Action Plan

Start defining actions you want to achieve and solve for the identified and prioritized needs. And before you put your plans into action, empower your program and project managers to execute those plans. Doing this is critical—not doing so can impede a successful outcome. For example, these managers may have to repeatedly go to leadership to get direction for matters leadership could have previously empowered them to do. Depending on their frequency of doing this, this could bog down the project.

One final note: mid-size and large companies will have departmental action plans that align with a company-wide strategy.

## Words for the Wise: Why Proper Planning of Digital Transformation is Vital

In the same series of studies discussed at the end of the last chapter, this interesting statistic surfaced:

**49% of US Federally Funded IT projects are either poorly planned, poorly performing, or both.**

That's why proper planning, including thoroughly evaluating potential platforms before selection, is essential!

So, our advice is this: as a leader in your organization, thoroughly do research and follow this book's steps. By doing so, you'll more likely defy this statistic—Michael Cantu's process we've outlined in this book has been battle-tested repeatedly, through engagements with Fortune 10 and 100 companies, to name a few.

And if you need any help, we would be happy to help guide you through your journey.

*Reflection Questions:*

1. *What have been your top three planning challenges in the past?*

   _______________________________________

   _______________________________________

   _______________________________________

   _______________________________________

2. *What did you learn that sparks some ideas to avoid similar situations in the future?*

   _______________________________________

   _______________________________________

   _______________________________________

   _______________________________________

3. *What two or three things can you implement to improve your planning process?*

   _______________________________________

   _______________________________________

   _______________________________________

# Chapter 8

## Create the Right Team

***What You Will Learn in This Chapter:***

*How to:*

- *Determine the right skill mix for your team*
- *Define your approach for adding new team members*
- *Involve your team members in the interview process effectively*
- *Help ensure your new hires will be able to perform their assigned roles effectively*

It's essential for business leaders to have the right people in the correct positions to execute projects successfully. If this element is missing, your project could suffer. On the other hand, assigning employees to roles suited to their skill set will help accelerate your project forward and help avoid project shortfalls.

Let's discuss best-practice steps to create a team of excellence:

## 1. Assess Your Internal Human Capital

It's essential to determine the skill sets you need for your team to accomplish the plan. Ask yourself:

- What skills do they possess that are known and unknown to the business?

- What are the skill gaps around the existing requirements of the action plan?

Answering these questions is vital because as you're digitally transforming, you'll want to add people from outside your organization to address any skill set deficit you may have.

## 2. Determine How to Fill Skill Gaps

You can use one or two ways to add your team—either through a consulting firm or a direct-hire/augmentation firm. If you decide to go the consulting route, their people can work with your team to fill particular skill deficits. The same goes for the direct-hire or augmentation pathway.

Whichever path you choose, you're looking for people who can take the initiative to push your plan forward.

## 3. Conduct Interviews

Before you start, ensure a solid interview methodology with established objectives exists. Consider the following best practices:

### *Involve Your Team During Interviews*

Since you'll be bringing two groups together, your internal team should be involved in the interview process. Doing so is critical; otherwise, you could experience a mismatch of your team's required skill sets and personalities. Your goal is to assess the strengths and weaknesses of the interviewees jointly and for you to observe how they interact with your current team members.

The goal is to determine how the individuals will get along and meld together. If you do your due diligence, this can help set your project on the road to success.

Next, observe how your team members respond to the interviewees, particularly if the candidates have more knowledge in a particular area than your team members. It's also essential to gauge the reaction and response between the two, observing a specific individual's "Yes/No" quality. Finally, determine if there could be potential problems, such as a current team member feeling intimidated by an incoming person due to a knowledge gap in a particular area.

The other thing that will determine the success of your project is if the candidate can execute the task at hand. Ask yourself: will this person fulfill the skill set deficit we advertised in the job description? That's important because this will mitigate the redundancy of skill sets and ensure you hire the skills needed to execute the plan successfully.

After completing the interviews, it's best to get feedback from your team on the interviewees. It's crucial to get buy-in and your teams' opinions before making your final decision; otherwise, you could encounter lots of friction down the road between team members.

Getting that buy-in should eliminate a lot of the comments like: "this person doesn't meet what we need," "I didn't get any input in bringing this person on board," or "I don't even feel like they're a good part of our team."

Doing this is vital because you don't want anyone dropping out midway on your DX projects, making excuses for why they don't think the team can succeed. Ultimately, the team's success will rely upon the success of individual team members.

## See It in Action: How Celebrating Your Team's Quirks Really Works

Kathy recently talked with Michael about how following his advice (the steps above) has worked for him when developing teams. Here are Michael's thoughts:

"Over the years, I've followed the steps in this chapter with great success. I've learned this: people have to feel they can be themselves, that even their differences and different skills are valuable—that their contributions are directly impactful to the whole.

"I've encouraged people on my teams to be themselves and be open to others—about who they are and what matters most to them. As a result, I've found that these teams become more quickly integrated and better equipped to value differences and appreciate others.

"This ability to accept others drives the project and team success. I've seen it repeatedly work over the years—whether it was working on a project for Microsoft, Jack Henry & Associates, or UnitedHealth Group.

"Here's an example: the UnitedHealth Group's stakeholders told us: 'This was one of the most successful projects we've seen in over 20 years.' That is owed entirely to the flexibility and openness of our team towards equal and accountable contributions."

For the above reasons, establishing this acceptance of others is foundational to project success. As a business leader, we encourage you to keep reading because you'll learn more strategies to help your organization successfully navigate your DX journey.

**Please Note: If you jumped into this chapter to learn more about teambuilding before finishing <u>Chapter 7</u> (like we redirected you), go back and read it. If you can learn these best practices for project planning, this will be an excellent foundation for executing your plan, which we'll discuss next.**

*Reflection Questions:*

1. What have been your top three challenges around establishing top-caliber teams?

___________________________________

___________________________________

___________________________________

___________________________________

2. What two or three things spoke to you while reading this chapter?

___________________________________

___________________________________

___________________________________

___________________________________

3. Of those two or three things, what is one you could implement to help solve your challenges?

___________________________________

___________________________________

___________________________________

___________________________________

# Chapter 9

## Executing the Plan

***What You Will Learn in This Chapter:***

- *The power of identifying roadblocks and their role in extending group vision*
- *How T-shirt sizing can help team members work to their strengths*
- *The importance of making adjustments to the plan for unforeseen circumstances*
- *The importance of using project velocity that can help establish a cadence of follow-ups and check-ins*

Many teams begin a new project with excitement, and along the way, become discouraged due to execution-related issues. When this happens, many problems can occur, such as slipping milestones and rising costs, to name a few. Unfortunately, this happens too frequently. As a business leader, your job is to set your project managers and leaders up for success.

So, how do you avoid such issues? Let's talk about best-practice steps for implementing your plan that, when followed, will help you keep on track.

Here are four key steps to executing a plan:

1.  Establish Group Vision
2.  Review the Plan
3.  Make Alterations
4.  Set Project Kickoff and Start Cadence

## 1. Establish Group Vision

After you bring the two groups together, start with the following questions:

- What are your objectives? What are you looking to accomplish?

- What are the problems or roadblocks that could surface?

This last point deserves in-depth attention, so let's dive into that.

### *Identify the Roadblocks*

Your team must have the opportunity to voice potential roadblocks at the very beginning without fear of being punished. Create a safe environment where members can be transparent and collaborate more effectively.

If people don't feel safe identifying potential roadblocks, or for some reason they can't identify issues, the team will typically run into problems later on down the road. If you've done an excellent job of creating that safe environment, and they're unwilling to share their thoughts, it could mean this—they're not thinking through the problem they're looking to solve. Every plan has issues or roadblocks you'll encounter, so diving deeper into their reluctance is a good tactic.

For these reasons, active listening and creating a safe environment play a significant role in helping to ensure success.

### *Using Roadblocks to Extend Group Vision*

Uncovering roadblocks is also beneficial for extending group vision. It comes down to looking at the following:

- Available resources

- The amount of time required to accomplish a task

- The quality level you've defined

As a rule of thumb, having less time will require more resources. If your timelines are short, you'll be able to compensate from different areas. When working with a smaller budget, you'll have to approach the problem together as a team uniquely. Clarifying time and budget constraints upfront helps the team identify current roadblocks and operate more efficiently.

These roadblocks can either be known or unknown. In many cases, the known roadblocks are always top-of-mind. Say, for instance, your team has needed to analyze a data set for quite a while. If they've previously defined the pre-existing parameters, they could quickly determine whether or not something is truly attainable.

Here's an example for unknowns. Your team has been working on a project with many unknowns, but the timeline for project completion is short. In this case, they may need to use creativity when bringing together data sets.

Here's another important point: every compensation for a roadblock often leads to other compensating behaviors, so it's best to have a clear picture of all items—while cultivating that safe environment we mentioned earlier. Doing so helps ensure everyone understands the objectives and the probability of achieving them. This clarity helps increase the likelihood of project success.

In the end, everyone should know the objective and the timeline. Uncovering roadblocks can help elevate what needs to happen, contributing to a solid project plan and corresponding vision.

## 2. Review the Plan

This aspect involves looking over the plan and ensuring the best use of your team's resources. From a software development perspective, a way to start is talking through the tasks you want to accomplish through T-shirt sizing.

### *T-Shirt Sizing*

When looking at the smaller units of your plan, ask each team member:

- Is this task a small, medium, or large item?

- Why do you think it's small, medium, or large?

For example, you may have a particular feature of your DX roadmap assigned to John on the team; however, he may not be the most competent to do that task.

In this example, John may say it's a large size, while everyone else in the group thinks it's a small or medium. His "large" assessment points out that someone else on the team could potentially finish it much quicker than he could. That way, you can give John another task that is a small or medium item.

The goal is to have the team working to their strengths. That's the benefit of this exercise. It's an excellent way to quickly figure out who will be the best fit for the task at hand.

### 3. Make Alterations

After you've ensured the capabilities within the team, it's best to make alterations to the plan to include unforeseen items, which is often the case. New things will arise once you start executing the project because your brains didn't go down those particular pathways when you first developed it.

For instance, you may have some legacy systems you didn't consider part of the original scope that interact or interfere with the process. It's best to escalate those issues to a business stakeholder, letting them know about the change.

Also, an unforeseen task might crop up mid-project, requiring an adjustment. It could be a newly identified required skill set or perhaps someone's on medical leave. This situation could be problematic if that skill set or the on-leave person is on the critical path.

So, it's necessary on occasion to make alterations such as these. But, while doing so, it's helpful to look for secondary or deviating pathways that are non-critical to get around those particular items.

## 4. Set Project Kick-Off and Start Cadence

This step involves setting a healthy cadence of follow-ups and check-ins based on the plan, team member assignments, and the sizings you've put together.

It would be best to tie this cadence to the project's velocity based on your resources and the project constraints you've established.

For example, if you have four team members on a project and know that they can work 40 hours a week over three months, your velocity is 160 (4 weeks x 40 hours = 160) for the month per person.

Velocity is essential because it will clue you in on what's crucial, what tasks you need to remove, and whether you can meet the actual deadlines.

In the end, following all these steps and ideas will help you be well on the way to executing a successful project!

**Words for the Wise: Execute Like an Expert**

It's helpful that you, as a leader in your organization, keep the following in mind:

Every day when working through plan execution, it's an assessment and reassessment of how you are performing to the plan. It involves check-ins with people to determine if they have the proper resources, among other considerations.

Knowing how your team's doing at all times will help keep them on track. Then, you'll pivot as needed, which hopefully won't be as frequent as check-ins.

By performing your due diligence, you'll execute a plan and stay consistent with a cadence that will help ensure your project is successful.

Now let's discuss how to measure success.

**Reflection Questions:**

1. What three execution challenges have you encountered on previous IT projects?

_________________________________

_________________________________

_________________________________

_________________________________

2. What hasn't worked for you to solve them?

_________________________________

_________________________________

_________________________________

_________________________________

3. What two or three things mentioned in this chapter can you implement to more successfully execute your projects?

_________________________________

_________________________________

_________________________________

_________________________________

# Chapter 10

## Measuring Success

Once you've implemented your plan, it's essential that you, as a business leader, measure the success of your efforts along the way; otherwise, how will you know if you're meeting your goals? And if you cannot do so, how will you know when to make midstream corrections? Not having this capability will, more often than not, negatively impact your probability of success.

How to effectively do this differs depending on numerous variables for each company. These include:

- The type of business

- The capital they have to invest

- Realistic timelines to accomplish their work

- Resources the company has to allocate

- The existing environment in which they operate

- Level of technical debt they have

Even so, the best measure of success is often the answer to the following question:

**Did the project meet the identified objectives and expectations?**

Let's back up a bit. Before you can even answer this question, you'll need to establish these objectives. There are several things you'll want to take into account.

First, it's best to determine the project's tangible and intangible success criteria. There are three areas, or factors, to consider. Your:

- People

- Processes

- Resources

There are other factors as well: financial, governmental, and environmental. But, for now, let's look at the top three:

## 1. People

There are several aspects to measuring success with the People resource. You can start by answering the following questions:

- Consider the well-being of your employees before and after the project.

  - Has there been an improvement in this area?

- Have you improved processes to gain efficiencies and created the ability to quickly on- and off-board people for the new workflow piece?

- Has the new process affected the end-users positively or negatively?

  - A way to validate this is upfront business process planning, which involves interacting with employees performing current roles and forecasting what those roles will look like moving forward.

- Are your stakeholders feeling optimistic about the way the project is transitioning?

This last question is critical; overall acceptance of the future state is essential for success once the transition is complete. You may meet all your integration goals, but true success lies with widespread acceptance. If end-user acceptance doesn't happen, then there is no success.

## 2. Process

The Process factor refers to the initial efficiency and effectiveness goals you identified. Once the project is complete, ask yourself these questions:

- Were your goals met?

- Does the pre-existing Roles Matrix look like the future state now?

- Was the projected efficiency impact met post-implementation?

Knowing these answers is invaluable! For instance, if your answers were less than favorable, this could indicate a need to revisit what you've implemented. Perhaps you could make further improvements to get closer to better results.

## 3. Resources

This factor comes down to an impact that is both tangible (money) and intangible (time). So, when reviewing your resource goals, here are some questions to ask:

- What was the monetary impact of the particular project?

- Was there a time or throughput improvement?

- Did you finish the project on time and within budget?

This last question is the most significant success factor. A deeper dive into the results could yield lessons learned that you can apply to future projects. That leads to the following discussion point.

## The Importance of Feedback Loops

Measuring outcomes is optimal when all three factors—People, Process, and Resource—are integrated to create feedback loops. Doing so helps ensure the lessons learned translate into future digital design and change workflows within the organization, increasing your likelihood of achieving more positive outcomes in the future. When organizations do this, it can become an overarching recipe for success.

For example, you might receive feedback that you could have used better process analysis on the project, which, if done correctly, would have lessened automation rework. Likewise, if you had had a more in-depth conversation with an employee about their role before the project, that would have decreased rework.

Implementing feedback like this on future projects can result in other benefits—better forecasting of the People, Process, and Resource factors. That, in turn, brings you back to square one—an increased ability to stay on track with budget and schedule.

When it's all said and done, ensuring you have a robust methodology in place to measure success will help an organization get better at everything they do, over and over again.

And as a business leader, who doesn't want that!

**See it In Action: Remote Work—Simplified.**

Are you interested in hearing some more DX success stories?

Then check out an interview with Michael Cantu of **Accelerate** in the next chapter. He talks about his experience and how workflow automation can make remote work a much more accessible, more efficient process.

*Reflection Questions:*

1. *How effective are your current measurement systems of project success?*

_______________________________________

_______________________________________

_______________________________________

_______________________________________

2. *What did you learn that helped spark some ideas to improve what you currently have?*

_______________________________________

_______________________________________

_______________________________________

_______________________________________

3. *Of those ideas, what is one you can implement on future projects?*

_______________________________________

_______________________________________

_______________________________________

_______________________________________

# Chapter 11

## How to Make Remote Working More Like a Day at the Beach

How many of you experience multiple challenges while working remotely?

Are you frequently missing the necessary resources at your fingertips when you need them?

How many of you are wishing for a day at the beach instead?

Remote work was undoubtedly a challenge during the height of the COVID pandemic; for many, that's still the case. Many employees have experienced the reality of repeatedly emailing multiple people for multiple reasons instead of running down the hall to talk to them. Or if something needs to be signed, they'll have to scan a document, upload it and send it off. More often than not, they've experienced all of the above multiple times!

The following interview with Michael Cantu of **Accelerate** happened during the COVID pandemic. He discusses a cost-effective solution, his **Accelerate** platform, that makes remote working a much more accessible, more productive way of doing business.

Using it may not compare to a day at the beach, but it could prove more enjoyable than your status quo.

**Kathy:** Thanks for joining me, Michael. First of all, what is **Accelerate** software?

**Michael:** It's workflow automation software that connects disparate systems, people, data, content, and workloads to accelerate your workforce. It streamlines your work, enabling you to have what you need to do your job at your fingertips to do it more effectively and efficiently.

**Kathy:** That sounds like it would be perfect to have right now during the COVID pandemic, especially with so many employees who have to work remotely. And I know there are significant benefits to this software. So what would you say are the top four?

**Michael:** The first thing I would say is—

## 1. Increased Productivity

These days, many people work in siloed IT systems that don't communicate well with each other and are expensive to integrate. So, we've focused on creating a platform that easily connects to other systems.

Here's a good example: Many new employees not only have the enormous challenge of learning how to do their jobs but also must know how to operate all the different systems and remember their login credentials. In addition, most people are working out of their email. So we've connected all these systems, bringing the work and work items together so the employee can accomplish their work using only one interface.

Post-implementation, our clients' employees now have everything at their fingertips in one system to do their job. It makes learning much more straightforward, and even longer-tenured employees can experience higher satisfaction levels.

That's been our experience with our clients. And that leads to the second benefit:

## 2. Better Customer Experiences

The advantages of workflow automation are evident from a customer experience perspective. It allows businesses to quickly communicate with customers and provide relevant information when they need it. Automation tools with responsive user interfaces also improve customer experience by providing immediate answers to their concerns and queries.

Workflow automation also enables accessible information as required. For instance, mobile-friendly forms offer customers convenience while reducing employee administrative tasks.

Automated data entry also saves time and provides consistent services while minimizing errors.

As so often is the case, happier employees often lead to better customer experiences.  Here's a good example.

Sometimes you need to call someone who owes you something to find out where they're at in the process so you can make a decision. We've all been there. That's one nice thing about **Accelerate**—the visibility into where things are going in the process.

For instance, a customer calls to find out the status of an order. With **Accelerate**, you can drill down to that order, find out who's handling it, and chat with the responsible person in real-time—using one system. You can be fast and consistent with your customers and, at the same time, hold employees accountable for their actions. Your customers see you as people that can be consistent, so when they need something, they get it. I think that is the best and the most phenomenal part of **Accelerate**.

**Kathy:** Yes, that sounds great! I know I'd be pleased if I could find out something right away about what's happening, especially if I were a disgruntled customer.

So what's another benefit of **Accelerate**?

**Michael:** I would have to say—

## 3. More Effective and Efficient Remote Working

We've created a solution that will empower an organization's employees to master the art of working remotely. We often spend too much effort going back and forth with email, and work can be disjointed. With this new platform, project managers can allocate work. Employees can schedule their daily tasks, and the system auto-assigns them to employees. The system will also send text notifications for high-priority items. With this new platform, you can log in and see what you need to complete for the day. **Accelerate** provides all the information you need at your fingertips.

You can also create customizable dashboards with the most critical metrics in minutes. Furthermore, you can drill down into high-level views of the data to determine a particular employee's performance over a defined timeline. That way, only objective data is used to gauge employee performance.

Companies with daily stand-ups can even do away with them (if desired) because task accomplishment is visible to everyone. Once you take on any work in the system, you can communicate with everyone involved with that work item as it progresses. It makes working outside the office a whole lot easier.

**Kathy:** I think that would be just amazing for remote workers because it's been new for many people. It would be wonderful to boot up your computer in the morning and see what you need to accomplish that day in **Accelerate**! That would be amazing. I can see how this would improve productivity and, in turn, overall customer experience.

Could you give an example of some work you've done for a client that has improved productivity and ultimately created happy customers?

**Michael:** Sure. We have clients in the transportation, finance, and healthcare fields. They are in the areas of compliance management. For example, one healthcare company we work with has to track audits within their company. They also need to report regularly to their state office.

Before their **Accelerate** implementation, there were many manual steps in tracking their 50-60 audits per month—managing 100s of texts and emails, manually filling out compliance forms, scanning them, and creating digital files.

With **Accelerate**, they now have an automated audit tracking workflow. Everybody logs into a system and sees what they need to see when they need to see it. The platform quickly creates electronic files for prompt submission to the state. You can even see all of the compliant audits versus the noncompliant audits. They can also see how things are progressing for all their audits.

Post-implementation, this company experienced a half-time job reduction in workload. The staff now spends more time improving the cultural life of the organization instead of tracking down audits and paper trails that don't directly add value to the overall experience.

That's a testimony of what **Accelerate** can do with compliance management.

Another area is medical billing. This project resulted in a reduction of a four-person to a one-person workload for this one company. In some areas, they have entirely removed tasks. These efficiency gains have allowed them to shift employees to take on higher-volume items.

In both cases, this doesn't mean they've laid off or will lay off people. Instead, they can take on more sales and grow their companies.

**Kathy:** Wow, that sounds phenomenal! I'm sure customers are reaping the benefit of the improved productivity.

What's another benefit that **Accelerate** can provide?

**Michael:** there are two that are closely related—

## 4. Quicker Implementations and Increased Ability to Innovate

With **Accelerate**, we can more quickly roll out automated workflows to our clients to fix their problems. With a no-code platform, we can develop a prototype of potential solutions so our clients can see what they will get before they invest their dollars.

Another thing we see is an increased ability for companies to innovate based on the lower costs and quicker time frames they're experiencing with **Accelerate** implementations. We also see that companies who want to innovate through software solutions need no longer put off potential projects. We've been able to help some organizations quickly implement projects that were at the bottom of their wish list. As a result, they're getting a bigger bang for their buck. I think that's a theme we'll see more in the future.

**Kathy:** That makes sense. So, here's our last question: Do you have more examples of how you've saved money for your clients?

**Michael:** Yes. We've seen this with non-software development firms: when considering investing in a software solution, they have to ask themselves this question: "Do I want to build and own my software, or should I license an existing platform?" Of course, it depends on what their needs are. If it falls within our wheelhouse, we've seen the value in licensing our software for what it brings to a customer.

For instance, one of our clients received a bid of ~$1M for a custom software development project. We came on the scene, and they selected us because our bid was only $20K, plus license fees.

**Kathy:** That's incredible! That's a ridiculous amount of savings! So not only can you improve productivity, but you can give better customer experiences and enable more effective remote working. You do it all at a good value.

**Michael:** That's right.

**Kathy:** Well, even I learned some things today. I believe those reading this will appreciate what they've learned about **Accelerate**. Thanks for joining us, Michael.

**Michael:** My pleasure.

**Words for the Wise: Delaying Your Digital Transformation Journey Can Cost You $$$**

When thinking about undertaking DX initiatives, one final thing to consider is to realize it's a continuous process. A delay in getting started could be the biggest roadblock to your success, and it can cost you money in the end.

Many companies are starting their DX journeys now, so our advice to you, as a business leader, is not to fall behind. There's never been a better moment to get started than today.

**Reflection Questions:**

1.  *What three aspects of this interview sparked your thought process around DX?*

_______________________________

_______________________________

_______________________________

_______________________________

_______________________________

_______________________________

2.  *Of those three, which one appealed to you most when considering DX efforts?*

_______________________________

_______________________________

_______________________________

_______________________________

_______________________________

_______________________________

# Chapter 12

## Some Parting Advice

With so many DX providers out there, it can be challenging to know where to turn. With that in mind, here's our advice to you:

**1. Get Referrals from Trusted Sources**

Just searching for someone on the Internet is not always the best tactic. Instead, seek out those who are knowledgeable about DX. Then, ask them for several referrals and do your due diligence during your initial discussions.

**2. Choose a Digital Transformation Provider Who is Committed to Your Goals**

Here's an excellent example of what NOT to do.

Michael met with a guy recently, whom we'll call Joe. Joe was frustrated at their service provider. He called Michael to tell him that his DX project wasn't going well. He explained how his experience started with a quick sale. It wasn't a consultative conversation, nor did his service provider ever ask the question: "Do you even know where you want to go?" Joe wanted his service provider to teach and train him on the system, which didn't happen.

## 3. Be Careful Not to Go Down the Quick-Fix Route

The partnership between the client and the provider must translate into a positive experience and result for both parties; otherwise, your project could suffer. You don't want an undertaking to end as it did with Joe!

## 4. Have the Mindset That Digital Transformation Will Propel You Into the Future

The decisions you make today impact the decisions you're going to be able to make tomorrow. It's not that you can't change today's decisions in the future, but they're most likely going to cost you a lot more money. But if you make the correct decisions today, with due diligence, then options for change in the future will be more plentiful and less costly.

Michael and I hope you've enjoyed this book. We are honored that you took your valuable time to read it. We hope to have answered some of your questions and given you new insights into this exciting topic.

**Would you like to unlock even more game-changing DX insights? As a "thank you" for purchasing our book, we're**

offering exclusive access to a bonus web page that dives deeper into hot topics around DX.

To gain access, view the QR code using your mobile phone's camera and click on the link that appears when you do so. Or, type this link in your browser: bit.ly/NNDTBonusOffer.

**Contact info:**

Michael Cantu – mcantu@accelerate.app

Kathy Kent Toney – kathy@kent.solutions

# Author Biographies

**Michael Cantu** is the founder and CEO of **Accelerate Technologies**, a cloud-based product company that offers a unique no-code workflow automation platform called **Accelerate**. Accelerate uses artificial intelligence and machine learning to speed workflows across people, systems, and geographies with great results—his clients regularly experience a +300% increase in productivity. Michael has helped organize and develop multi-million-dollar platforms for organizations like UnitedHealth Group and 40% of US credit unions and banks. UnitedHealth Group said that the specialty pharmacy project he facilitated was one of the most successful IT projects they had seen in 20 years. Michael has an MBA from the University of Kansas and lives in Olathe, Kansas.

You can contact him at www.accelerate.app.

**Kathy Kent Toney** is the Founder and CEO of **Kent Business Solutions**, a process improvement services consulting firm. She is a certified Six Sigma Black Belt, Lean Professional, and Professional Scrum Master with over 35 years of

experience, with +20 years spent working in Fortune 100 companies, helping to optimize and streamline their operations. Her most significant achievement was facilitating a sales process that experienced an increase in sales from $85M to +$300M over nine years of its usage. This process was nationally recognized as best-in-class in this company's industry space. She is an Opinion Columnist for CEOWORLD Magazine and was recently honored as a Top 25 Thinkers360 Thought Leader and Influencer in Project Management. Kathy lives in the Kansas City, Missouri area, serving in her church as a worship leader and volunteering with a prison ministry.

You can contact her at www.kent.solutions.